MIRACLES OF GOD

and the Power of Prayer
My Journey from Brokenness to Healing
by

F. R. Shumake

I0210823

MIRACLES OF GOD AND THE POWER OF PRAYER

First edition. October 31, 2025.

Copyright © 2025 F.R. Shumake.

ISBN: 979-8999319913

Written by F.R. Shumake.

Table of Contents

Cover design by F. R. Shumake.

Miracles of God *and the power of prayer, my journey from brokenness to healing*
By F. R. Shumake

Foreword

Before you dive into the chapters of this book, let me say something as a friend who watched much of it unfold.

This isn't some feel-good story polished for inspiration. This is a life that was gutted and rebuilt—more than once. I watched Fred lose almost everything. I saw him go back and forth with addiction, spiral into darkness, and burn bridges he never thought he'd cross again. And then—I watched him crawl back with nothing but prayer and grit.

There were times I honestly didn't think he'd make it. But then something happened. Not all at once, but piece by piece, I saw a man who once felt too far gone start to believe again. He started listening for God's voice instead of his own. He began to let go of the pride, the excuses, and the pain—and grab hold of something greater.

This book is raw. It's uncomfortable. It's not for people who like tidy endings or fake smiles. But it's real. And more than anything, it's proof that the power of God and prayer is still alive.

So if you're feeling lost, or if someone you love is caught in that same cycle, keep reading. There's hope in these pages. And if God can work a miracle in Fred's life, He can do it in yours too.

— An Anonymous Friend

Preface

There are two things you need to know before you read a single chapter of this book:

First, I didn't write this to make myself look good. This is not a tale of a hero's journey—it's a story of human failure, divine mercy, and undeserved redemption. I wrote it for anyone who's ever wondered if they've gone too far, lost too much, or wasted too many chances. I wrote it because I've been there.

Second, this isn't fiction. Every story you'll read is real. Some parts are hard to revisit—moments I'm not proud of—but they're all part of what God has brought me through. I didn't survive by chance. I survived because prayer still works. Because miracles still happen. And because even when I wasn't looking for Him, God was looking out for me.

So, before you begin, ask yourself this: What if the worst thing you've ever been through could become the foundation of someone else's healing?

That's what this book is. It's not about who I used to be—it's about who I'm becoming, and who you can become too.

Acknowledgments

First and foremost, I thank God —

For never giving up on me, even when I gave up on myself. For the grace, the miracles, and the power of prayer that rescued me time and time again. This book exists only because of Your mercy, and I give You all the glory.

To my Grandma, Granddad, and my mom —

I thank you for the seeds of truth you planted in me as a child. I may have strayed far from the path, but your words never left me.

As Proverbs 22:6 says: "Train up a child in the way he should go, and when he is old he will not depart from it."

There were many years when I misunderstood what life was really about — but today, I see it clearly, and I know it was your foundation that brought me back.

To Dignity Health —

Thank you for connecting me to Lotus 24/7. That was the turning point.

To Placer County Adult System of Care, Action Team, Granite Wellness

AMI Housing / Harbor House,

California CalFresh and Medi-Cal —

Your support helped stabilize my life when I couldn't do it on my own. Each of you played a role in my recovery and rebuilding.

To Rick Wheeler's Recovery Now and my sponsor, Terry C —

Thank you for walking this journey with me, one day at a time.

To the Fellowship of Alcoholics Anonymous —

Your honesty, your strength, and your shared hope reminded me that I am not alone. You helped me see that healing is possible.

To Set Free Christian Fellowship and Pastor Ray "Weebles" Slocum —

Thank you for pouring into my spirit and reminding me that Jesus saves to the uttermost. Your ministry showed me what true surrender looks like.

Author's Note

I'm so grateful you've chosen to walk with me through these pages. Writing this book has been one of the hardest and holiest things I've ever done. I've had to revisit places in my life that I'd rather forget—but I did it because I believe the truth matters. Because I believe in the power of testimony.

I didn't write this to elevate myself. Quite the opposite—I wrote this to show how far down I went, and how far God was willing to reach to lift me out. These are eyewitness accounts of things I lived through. I don't know why I was allowed to survive some of them. Maybe God trusted that when I finally stepped outside of myself, I would carry the message forward. Maybe it's not about me at all—maybe it's about you, the one reading this now.

There were people who scoffed at me along the way. Some still do. They've said I'm trying to put myself above others. But that couldn't be further from the truth. My life has been broken, messy, and full of mistakes. What I'm trying to show isn't my strength—it's God's.

If even one person finds hope in these words, then all of it—the pain, the writing, the struggle to get it just right—it's worth it.

Thank you for letting me share my story with you.

—F. R. Shumake

Dedication

For Jeromy and Rebecca

Jeromy, you were the original inspiration for this book. I watched God work miracles in your life—miracles I never believed were possible for someone like me. For years, I thought God's healing was for other people, not for someone so broken, so far gone. But I was wrong. God was always working in my life, even when I couldn't see it.

Today, my heart aches because we don't speak. But I understand. I remember the pain I carried from my own childhood, and I know some wounds take time to heal. Still, not a day goes by that I don't think of you or your sister, Rebecca. I never stopped loving either of you. I just didn't know how to show it.

For so long, I drowned in regret, guilt, and shame. I ran. I numbed myself. I hurt people, including the ones I love most. But today, I don't want to live in that bondage anymore. I want to be free—to live honestly, to love deeply, and to rebuild what I once destroyed. I pray that God, in His perfect timing, will reconcile us.

This book is not an excuse for my actions, but it is my offering of truth and surrender. I dedicate it not only to you, Jeromy and Rebecca, but also to my family—especially my mom, Aunt Shirley, my cousins, my Grandma and Granddad—who never gave up on me. And to my friend Terry, whose kindness helped me believe again.

Most of all, I thank God, who never stopped reaching for me, even when I had nothing left to give.

Chapter 1: Before We Begin

Throughout my life, I've been riddled with addiction and alcoholism. I don't blame anyone else for it—I blame it on my own self-centeredness and selfishness, and the constant drive to be in a place of prestige. I always thought I was either better than other people or less than them. I never felt like I truly fit in. I was always searching for a way to feel equal with others, to open up and feel normal—but I never could. It was always one or the other: better than, or less than.

As my addictions got worse, I never wanted to admit defeat. I never wanted to admit that something had mastered me. I thought I could always regain control, rise above, prove I was stronger. But I was wrong.

The hardest thing for me to admit was that an inanimate object—alcohol or drugs—had more power over me than I did. When I finally admitted that, and sincerely asked God to step into my life and take control, that's when everything began to change.

I've had brief moments of sobriety before, but never like what I experience today. Life is wonderful now, because I've let God orchestrate it. It seems strange, I know—but one of the hardest things for a person to do is to give up control over their own life. And yet, that surrender is where peace begins.

I don't know all the good things that are still to come, but I do know this: good things are coming, because I've finally let go.

Looking back, I can see that God has always wanted good things for me. It didn't always look the way I thought it should, but I've come to realize that I don't even know what's best for me. I've always been drawn to the wrong things—shiny things. Sex. Drugs. Rock and roll. The grandiosity. The things that made me look like I had it together, like I was cool or a big shot. I wanted people to look up to me—because deep down, I felt awkward and weird around others.

But today, I don't need to wear a mask. I want to be approachable. I want to be someone others can talk to without feeling judged, less than, or intimidated. I still wrestle with my old expectations sometimes—I put them on other people and forget that not everyone is in the same place I am. Many are still suffering under those same pressures to act superior or hide their pain. But the truth is, we're all the same. We're all seeking the same things: love, joy, and peace.

I've always had some kind of strong spiritual connection with God. I don't know why that is. I don't know why me over others. Maybe it's because I've always had the heart of a child when it comes to faith. I've believed in the scriptures—and in what some might call "magic," but I call the power of God. I believe there is so much more to this world than we can see or understand. And I believe there are forces at work trying to keep us from tapping into that truth.

There are people who want to control others—for their own selfish or financial gain. They keep man from experiencing what we were created for: a relationship with God. A walk like Adam had in the garden. But in our selfishness and self-centered behavior, we've strayed from that relationship and placed ourselves at odds with God.

Still, He keeps reaching out.

God has shown Himself in my life through miracles—undeniable ones. The healing of my son. The reunification with my mom. Again and again, He has revealed Himself. And yet, in my blindness, I kept going, focused on my wants and needs, failing to recognize His hand.

Today, I let Him guide me. And I stand back in awe of the gifts He's given me.

I have a new understanding now—about humanity, about society, and about myself. I know the pain of loneliness. I know what it feels like to desperately want peace, to want that ticking in your head to stop. I know what it's like to want to sit in a room alone and not go mad—to look in the mirror and not feel disgust.

And I know this: God is there. And God is kind. He is not the condemning God so many imagine.

I hope in the pages of this book, you find something—some glimmer of hope that rekindles your spirit or sparks faith for the first time. If a full-blown junkie and alcoholic can find peace and healing, then it's proof that God's grace is real. That His power is real. And that it's waiting for you, too.

Just ask Him.

And I know—He will answer.

Chapter 2: The Promise

This chapter is dedicated to Buddy. I love you, Buddy.

I remember one day in 1997. I was working at an old man's house shortly after my wife and I had gotten married. I received a call from my wife urging me to call my Aunt Betty, who was hysterical. She couldn't quite make out exactly what was going on, but she knew it was bad. Asking the man if I could make a long-distance call, I proceeded to phone my Aunt Betty, who was in tears, begging me to come down. Something had happened with Buddy.

I asked, "What is going on?"

My aunt exclaimed, "He's gone!"

"What do you mean, he's gone? Was he in a car wreck or something? Did he have a heart attack?"

"No—he killed himself."

Immediately, I thought to myself, *Who the hell is this?*—as if it were some kind of prank call. I knew in my heart that Buddy didn't kill himself. He was the kind of person who was totally adamant against suicide. He didn't even like people joking about it. He nearly beat my ass one time when I joked about committing suicide. Grabbing me by the shirt and pulling me to his face, he said, "You don't even joke about that kind of shit! You deal with the hand that you were dealt. That's a pussy's way out!"

From that moment, I knew something wasn't right. I gathered my stuff, picked up my wife and kids, and we headed down to Calimesa.

When we arrived, Aunt Betty was a complete wreck. She had walked in and found her son sitting in the living room chair with a rifle between his legs. He had blown his brains out—right there in her living room. That alone told me something was off. My cousin Buddy would never have done something so painful to his mom, something so selfish as to leave himself like that for her to find.

Another thing: I knew he had a .45 caliber handgun. Who uses a rifle between their legs to commit suicide if they have a handgun? It didn't make sense. It never sat right with me. From the bottom of my heart, with every fiber of my being, I knew it wasn't true.

Sometime later, as I've described in another chapter, my wife and I had separated. I had been in Colorado working, then returned to California, full-blown in addiction again. I was a wreck.

Aunt Betty had gotten her third DUI and had to do some jail time. I was asked to stay at her house and take care of things while she was gone. It gave me a place to stay—I didn't have much besides my van and motorcycle. Grandma's house had already been sold, and the place we all knew as a refuge was gone.

During that time, I was partying a lot. One night, I had some friends over. A young girl came by—she was 18, and I was 30. I remember the first time she came over. We were all hanging out in the living room, and she asked where the bathroom was. I pointed it out. As she got up to walk down the hallway, she stopped with wide eyes, froze, turned around, and sat back down.

"I thought you needed to use the restroom?" I asked.

She replied, "No, I'll hold it."

I was confused. "What do you mean? The bathroom's right there."

She said, "No, I'll just hold it."

I had a suspicion but didn't say anything. I even walked to the hallway and turned on the bathroom and hall lights. "There's nothing to be afraid of," I told her.

She said, "No, I'll be all right."

I dropped the issue. Mind you—this was the same house where my cousin had supposedly shot himself. I never shared that with her. She had no knowledge of my family or what had happened in that room.

Over time, a relationship began between the two of us. I was trying to fill that hole inside me again. It fed my ego and my self-centeredness.

One night, around 2:00 a.m., we were lying in bed talking. Suddenly, she threw the covers over her head and started trembling.

"What are you doing?" I asked, thinking she was joking—but she wasn't. She was shaking.

"Nothing, I'm okay," she said.

"No, you're not. You're literally shaking. What's wrong?"

She hesitated. "You'll think I'm crazy."

"I won't. Tell me what's going on."

"There's somebody in the room with us."

I shot up and looked around—clear view of all four walls. No one was there.

"There's nobody here."

"Yes, there is. He's standing at the foot of the bed. He's trying to talk to you."

"Why can't I hear him or see him?"

"I don't know!" she yelled.

"What is he trying to say?"

"Shut up, it's hard to make out."

"Who is it?"

She replied, "Will. Will."

I asked, "Wilbur?"

She nodded. "He says yes."

"Wilbur Lamar? My cousin Buddy?"

"Yes," she confirmed.

First thing out of my mouth: "Did he do it?"

She answered, "He said no."

I clenched my fist and waved it in the air. "I knew it!"

I asked, "Who did? Was it this person? That person?"

She stopped me. "He doesn't want you to worry about that. He's okay. He wants to know if you remember the promise."

At that moment, my mind raced. That's why he came back.

There was a time when I was out in front of Grandma's house smoking dope. Buddy had been using too. We were both in dark places. I remember him grabbing the pipe out of my hand and hurling it into the street. I know he wanted to take a hit himself—but instead, he looked at me desperately.

"Raymond," he said, "promise me. Promise me that one day we're going to quit this stuff."

I looked him dead in the eye. "I promise you, Buddy. I don't know when—tomorrow, next month, or years from now—but I promise you, one day we will stop. I will stop."

I turned to the girl and asked, "You mean the promise Buddy and I made in front of Grandma's house? There was no one else around—just him and me."

She had no way of knowing that. None.

She truly saw him. Heard him. He was at the foot of the bed, trying to reach me.

Why some people are given that gift and others aren't, I don't know. But I am an eyewitness to this. I said, "Yes, I remember the promise," and he was gone.

I later showed her a photo of Buddy. She shuddered.

"That's him," she said. "That's who talked to me. That's who I saw that first night—I saw him standing in the hallway by the bathroom. That's why I didn't go."

God allowed him to reach me from beyond the grave. To remind me. Because he cared—not just about himself, but about *me.*

He had been murdered, but he came back because he was worried about my well-being.

People ask me if we're conscious after death. I say yes. Yes, we are.

My cousin loved me enough to send a message from the other side. And today, with tears in my eyes, I can say: Buddy, I'm keeping the promise.

I love you, Buddy. I'm in a good place now.

Thank you for your love—even from the grave.

I could go on about this for hours. I truly believe that loved ones who have passed watch over us. They care for us. They wait for us.

Why bad things happen? I don't know. I'm not God. I don't understand His reasons. I only know the truth of what I experienced.

This is my eyewitness account. It is 100% true.

Thank you, God, for allowing it.

I understand now—it's not my job to make people believe what I've seen. That's the Holy Spirit's work. He'll choose who to reveal it to.

But it *is* my responsibility to share it.

Just as I am in this book.

Chapter 3: Jeromy's Healing Story

I remember when my son was born—October 30, 1997. What a great day! I had a son. My wife and I had been free from addiction for quite some time, even though I had my occasional drinks and some infrequent drunkenness. Life was good, and we had a loving, caring relationship. I had a good job and was making good money.

About six or seven months into this job, I injured my back, which resulted in back surgery. I went on disability and spent most of my days at home, playing with my kids and videotaping them. My son Jeromy was almost a year old by then. He was a happy little guy. Very rarely did he cry—he was always laughing. He used to chase this little ball around the room, dragging himself along, pushing it and chasing it.

One day, I finally realized that was exactly what he was doing—using his arms to pull himself along, but not using his feet. Even though he could move his legs, he didn't rely on them at all. Trying to stand him up to get him to walk was impossible; even getting him to sit up was unachievable without propping him.

When my wife got home that day, I called her aside and said, "I think there's something wrong with Jeromy." She immediately ran over, picked him up, and inspected him. Looking at me, she asked, "What's wrong with him?" I said, "Nothing major—but I think it is major." Not like his well-being depended on it right at that moment, but I explained to her what I had been observing: that he didn't use his legs, only his arms.

She noticed it too, and we decided to take him to Loma Linda University—where he was born—to have some tests done. We did so, and after all the official tests were taken, we waited for the diagnosis.

We were both astonished and heartbroken to receive the news: the doctors determined that he had cerebral palsy; that the gray matter was not developing in his brain. My wife, especially, was devastated.

I couldn't help but think in my mind—I knew exactly the night he was conceived, and we were high as a kite. At the time, we had been smoking meth—both of us in the midst of our full-blown addiction.

It was silent in the car most of the way home. As we approached the house, the gravity of the situation weighed upon us, and we began to discuss things. When we got inside, my wife was in tears. She exclaimed, "What can we do?"

The only answer I had for her was that there was nothing we could do—except pray. There was no cure for cerebral palsy, and as far as I know, there still isn't. But there is one who has all authority—and that is God. The scriptures say that God holds the king's heart in His hand and can direct him whichever way He wills. So why would this situation be any different? He is the Chief Physician and Healer.

So that's what we did. We prayed.

I don't remember the exact prayer that my wife and I said that day, but I do remember the prayer I said alone afterward. I quietly went out into the backyard, bowed my head, and stood before God. Broken inside, I pleaded:

"If there is anything I did that has created this problem with my son, please take it away. Please don't let my son suffer for choices that I've made in my life. Please let him have a normal life like I did—to learn right from wrong, to go through life and make his own choices and experience the consequences or blessings thereof. But by no means do I want my son to suffer because of my iniquities."

And I left that at the feet of God.

In my upbringing, I was aware of the church and many types of faith, and I was convinced that there are powers out there—unexplainable—and that certain individuals are given the gift to heal. I didn't know of one off-hand, but I figured someone in the congregation at Calvary Chapel (now Joshua Springs Calvary Chapel in Yucca Valley) might have that gift.

My wife and I approached Pastor Gerald, gave him the information verbally, and asked if the congregation could lay hands on Jeromy and pray for him. He inquired about documentation. He said, "The last thing I'm going to do is have a sideshow here at my congregation," which I fully agreed with. Upon presentation of the documentation, he agreed and said we could extend an invitation for prayer after the second service that Sunday. He made it clear that we only wanted people who were willing to stay—we didn't want to hold anyone hostage. That was sound judgment—truly, the wisdom of God and Christ dwelled within him.

That following Sunday, as planned, the invitation was given. We brought Jeromy to the front of the sanctuary and handed him to Pastor Gerald. My wife and I stood there, with my daughter and stepdaughter at her side. Both of us were sobbing, reflecting on our drug addiction and the things that may have caused Jeromy's condition.

As Pastor Gerald began to pray, people reached out to touch my wife, my son, and me. There were whispers in the background—other prayers going up. Some were in tongues; others were spoken clearly. The power I felt was unmistakable. There was something there.

There were no flashes of light. My son didn't do cartwheels. But something good—something powerful—was in that place.

As we wiped our tears and turned around, there were over a hundred people still standing in the sanctuary. The other two hundred had gone on their way, which I hold no resentment toward. But I am so thankful for those who stayed and were willing to take part.

God is my witness—my son was standing up within two weeks. I don't know whether it was the laying on of hands, our joint prayer, or my prayer alone. I believe it was all of it—and the sincerity behind it. I had no selfish intent. I wanted Jeromy to be healed because I felt my selfishness had caused his affliction.

Maybe a month after the diagnosis—and two weeks after he began standing—a county-appointed nurse came to visit. The county sends a nurse every quarter to check on children with needs like his. I believe we were still receiving AFDC or family assistance at the time.

When she walked up to the door and saw Jeromy standing behind the screen, she looked around for other children and said, almost in disbelief, "Is this the same baby you brought down for diagnosis?"

We laughed and said, "Yes, that's him."

She replied, "Oh my God—what happened?"

We invited her in and explained everything that had transpired since we returned home. Even though she worked at a Seventh-day Adventist or Christian university facility, I don't think she fully grasped or believed what had happened.

And truly—that's none of my business.

I know what happened. God healed my son.

In reflection, though I am eternally grateful, I still wonder why my son and not other children? I cannot pretend to imagine the heartache that some parents must have in similar situations. Praying earnestly for God's healing power or Mercy and yet getting no resolve. The only thing I can hold true to is that I never blamed God for my son's infirmities, but I did and do praise Him for taking them away.

Even though these events were true and powerful, they still didn't override the selfishness and self-centeredness within me—and shortly after this miracle, my wife and I separated.

Chapter 4: The Resentment

As far back as I can remember—which was pretty young—I remember being in diapers and my mother rocking me back and forth in the living room. It was evening, and I could see the reflection of the TV off of her glasses. I remember the moment so well. I couldn't have been more than two years old—I was just learning how to talk. My great-grandmother had been in the house with us for some time, and then, all of a sudden, she was gone. I remember asking my mom, "Where is Great Grandma?"

My mom replied, "She's gone, honey."

I said, "Well, where did she go?"

"She went to be with Jesus," she said.

"So... are we ever going to see her again?"

"Yes, one day we will be with her in heaven with Jesus."

I asked, "What are we going to do there?"

And my mom said, in a sweet baby voice to help me understand, "We are going to live forever and ever and ever."

She was obviously trying to emphasize how long forever was to a little child.

Instantly, a wave of fear came over me as I tried to wrap my little mind around the idea of forever. I remember the fear it instilled in me—and even today, as an adult, if I truly go back to that moment or try to fathom forever in my mind, I can feel that same fear bubbling up. It's something too powerful for humans to fully understand, I believe—the infinite, the unknowing, no beginning, no end. I cannot grasp the concept, I believe all those things will be revealed at the time of my death here on Earth. All things will be revealed.

The year had to have been 1973. I still remember being in diapers, walking around the house barefoot, when one day Mel and Mary came over to visit. All the adults were gathered around the kitchen table talking—that was the main gathering place in our house—while I was left to the devices of the old black-and-white Zenith TV in the living room.

Curious as to what was going on in there, I strolled into the kitchen and climbed up on Mel's lap. Sitting there on his knee, sucking my thumb and kicking my feet, I remember feeling like I was big stuff—because I was sitting on my dad's lap.

All of a sudden, the room went quiet. I looked around at everyone's faces—they were all looking at me and Mel. I turned and looked at Mel's face. The sheer contempt and disgust in his eyes, and the dialogue that followed, scarred me for years. It filled me with feelings of rejection, worthlessness, and a kind of internal loneliness I can't fully describe. But I'm sure some readers know exactly what I'm talking about.

Turning back to my mom, she began to coax me off his lap.

She said, "Now get down, honey."

I said, "But I want to sit on my daddy's lap."

She said, "Well... that's not your daddy."

Perplexed, I replied, "But he's Lemie's daddy," which was true—Mel was the father of my half-brother.

She answered, "Yes, that is Melvin Lee's dad, but that's not your dad."

Once again confused, I asked, "Well, where's my daddy?"

My mom reached out and said, "I'll explain that to you when you're old enough to understand."

And that's how the conversation would go every time I brought it up.

This only added to the pain. It made me think that I wasn't smart enough to understand. But I never told her how I felt. I just kept it all bottled up.

I remember going out to Blythe, California, with my grandparents. We had a piece of property out there with a mobile home. My aunt and uncle lived there with their four boys. I loved visiting, because I could play with kids my age. Scott, the youngest, was only a couple of months younger than me. We had a great time getting into mischief, digging in the sand, chasing lizards—just doing the things boys do. We explored and dreamed big.

It was a long drive between Blythe and Calimesa, California—a small town on Interstate 10 near San Bernardino and the foothills of Big Bear.

My mom had been left in charge of feeding the cat and watching the house while we were gone. That was common. My mom was in and out of my life throughout my adolescence. I didn't understand why.

But as we pulled into the driveway, I had a sinking feeling that she wouldn't be there when we got back. And sure enough, she was gone.

I immediately ran to my room—and saw that my piggy bank was missing. I knew it had been there when I left. I knew she had taken it.

A feeling came over me, and I knew where to look. I went through the gate into the vacant field behind the house—and there it was, smashed into tiny pieces. All the money was gone, including the single dollar bill my daddy George had given me.

I was heartbroken. It wasn't about the coins or the fact that my mother was gone—it was about that dollar bill daddy George had given me. My daddy George was a real cowboy from Texas who broke broncos until he was 80 years old. He had a long history as a cattleman going back to 1900 and was even featured in a book called *Face of a Cowboy*, which is well known in Texas.

He had come to live with us for the last five years of his life, because he could no longer care for the ranch. He passed away at age 92. At that time, he was my idol.

But at the same time, I was deeply hurt that my mom had taken that money—and run off. I think it was at that moment that the resentment truly took root. That was the moment the line was drawn in my heart between my mom and me.

Continuing with my mom—I think I was around 10 years old when she finally told me that my dad's name was Gary. She said they had met in San Diego, dated for a while, and that's how I was conceived. According to her, things didn't work out and there were problems with where she would stay. That's why I ended up staying with my grandparents and why they adopted me at age seven.

I reluctantly accepted this as the truth. But deep down, I still carried resentment—especially because she never mentioned the piggy bank, never apologized, and had lied so many times before.

Years later, I entered the Second Chance program while in jail. For the first time in my life, I was taught how to deal with my feelings without drugs or alcohol. I was introduced to the program of AA again and how to actually apply it to my life.

Looking back now, I realize I only tapped into maybe 20% of that program. But I was given tools—tools to talk about my feelings. I remember telling my mom that I forgave her. We talked about my dad again, and she held firm to the same story. I accepted it has truth.

This was 1993.

Some years later, I got married. We had a daughter and a son. We lived in Joshua Tree, and I had the best job I'd ever had—working as a laborer and equipment operator. I was making good money. Then I hurt my back, and the rug was pulled out from under me. I was at home on disability, playing with my kids, videotaping them. Despite the hardships, there were joyful moments—moments most fathers don't get to witness because they're away at work.

One day I was watching Ricki Lake of all things. The topic was genealogy. I became curious about my roots. I had copper-red hair; my mom had jet-black hair. So I figured my dad must have been of Scottish or Irish descent.

So I made the call.

I had a good relationship with my mom at the time, although it was rocky—my wife and her didn't always get along.

I said, "Hey Mom, I was watching this thing on TV about genealogy. You know I've never really wanted to meet my dad—and I still don't. I don't believe in just dropping a bomb in someone's life, knocking on a stranger's door and saying, 'Hey, I'm your son.' But I do want to know what his last name was—just to know my roots."

There was a long silence.

Then my mom said, "I don't know, son."

My heart sank. And there was a long pause. Reluctantly I asked, already knowing the answer, "Do you even know his first name?"

There was more silence.

"No," she whispered.

The unthinkable had become reality.

Everything she'd ever told me about telling the truth, about how "the truth will always serve better than a lie"—all of it came crashing down. My blood boiled. The resentment have you had been rekindled and fanned into flames and erupted inside me.

As calmly as I could say,

I told her, "Mom... I love you. I think I do. I'm supposed to. I'm supposed to respect my elders. But I'm tired of playing this fucking game with you. I can't tell you when the next time will be that I talk to you... but I just can't do this anymore. Have a nice life."

And I hung up.

That was 1998.

In 2005, I earned the "privilege" of going to the state penitentiary—ironically speaking, of course. My drinking and drugging had taken me to rock bottom again. I lost my union job. Then I made the brilliant decision to steal a car and flee to Mexico, trying to escape my problems.

I ran out of money. Big problem.

Then someone said, "Hey gringo, I know where you can make some money." What an idiot I was.

So I started smuggling across the border. I got caught in San Ysidro with 50 kilos—just before marijuana became legal in California—and was sentenced to 16 months.

While I was in George Bailey Detention Center in San Diego, waiting to catch the chain to R.J. Donovan Reception Facility, I was reading my Bible on commissary night. I turned to Matthew chapter 18.

The Parable of the Unmerciful Servant (Matthew 18:21–35, NIV):

Then Peter came to Jesus and asked, "Lord, how many times shall I forgive my brother or sister who sins against me? Up to seven times?"

Jesus answered, "I tell you, not seven times, but seventy-seven times.

Jesus did not state this as an actual number of times that we should forgive but to emphasize that we should always forgive.-

Therefore, the kingdom of heaven is like a king who wanted to settle accounts with his servants. As he began the settlement, a man who owed him ten thousand bags of gold was brought to him. Since he was not able to pay, the master ordered that he and his wife and his children and all that he had be sold to repay the debt.

At this the servant fell on his knees before him. 'Be patient with me,' he begged, 'and I will pay back everything.' The servant's master took pity on him, canceled the debt and let him go.

But when that servant went out, he found one of his fellow servants who owed him a hundred silver coins. He grabbed him and began to choke him. 'Pay back what you owe me!' he demanded.

His fellow servant fell to his knees and begged him, 'Be patient with me, and I will pay it back.' But he refused. Instead, he went off and had the man thrown into prison until he could pay the debt.

When the other servants saw what had happened, they were outraged and went and told their master everything that had happened.

Then the master called the servant in. 'You wicked servant,' he said, 'I canceled all that debt of yours because you begged me to. Shouldn't you have had mercy on your fellow servant just as I had on you?'

In anger his master handed him over to the jailers to be tortured, until he should pay back all he owed.

"This is how my heavenly Father will treat each of you unless you forgive your brother or sister from your heart."

As I read the last line, I didn't hear it audibly—but inside my head, I heard the voice of God, distinct and undeniable.

He said, "You hypocrite. Your mother is dying and alone because of the resentment you hold in your heart against her. And yet, you do the same thing to your own children."

I was crushed.

That realization—an epiphany—was overwhelming. I tried to hold back my emotions, but it burst like a breached dam. I grabbed my military blanket and stuffed it into my mouth so no one would hear me scream and sob in shame. It must have lasted five minutes before I could even remotely contain myself.

When I finally pulled the blanket away, I saw it—it was so faint but it was there. The Spirit of an eagle, carrying a stone, flew away from me and soared through the jailhouse window. It passed through the day room and out of the jail, through the outer wall.

In that moment, I knew: I had forgiven my mom.

I no longer held resentment. I no longer held anger. I loved her. I knew she had done what she thought was right at the time.

It was gone.

I can't describe how light I felt. In the blink of an eye, I realized that all the counselors in my past were right. That my relationships with women were deeply affected because of that resentment that I held against my mother, but I also realized it wasn't just with women, it was with everyone. My friends, my family. They were all affected. All my relationships affected because of that resentment that I held against my mom.

From that moment forward, I made it my mission to find my mom... and reconcile.

Chapter 5: The Reunification

Upon my release from state prison in mid-March of 2006, I had determined that I was going to go to San Diego to find my mom and reconcile with her. I had never lived in San Diego before except for when I was an infant, times that I vaguely remember but still have fleeting memories of those times.

The economy had been very high just prior to my incarceration, and I had been working for the operating engineers, a job that I had always dreamed about having, only to be fired from it. I figured that if I paroled to San Diego that I could still work for the operating engineers, and being San Diego, I figured there was plenty of work. Unfortunately, while I was locked up, the economy took a crap, and I went from being on the B-list as a grade setter to 450-something on the C-list. That was not good.

I had established room and board already, just a little bit inland somewhere around 52nd Street. Knowing the time would be coming for rent again—because 30 days rolls around very quickly—I set out on the endeavor to find employment. I remember going to several different agencies, and going business to business, but not too many people were keen on hiring a parolee.

Even though I had had the epiphany with God, I still had the addictive mind and personality and had not done anything in that aspect of my life for personal recovery or addiction treatment. There was a liquor store right around the corner and alcohol was very easy to get. I began drinking again, then found out people within the house were smoking crack cocaine, and soon I became dependent upon that one more time.

I was still struggling with grandiosity, thinking more of myself than I should have, thinking that I deserved a high-paying job. And I wrestled with these things in my mind. When I had to take on a low-paying labor job sweeping up trash at construction sites, I didn't view it as a job and a way to make money or away to make ends meet—it was all surrounded about my social stature.

As I became familiar with my surroundings, the day came up that I set out to find my mother. I remember waking up early that day and leaving the house about 7:00. I got on the bus and set out to her last known residence. It was a board-and-care facility that my wife and I had gone and visited her with the kids when Tina was pregnant with Jeromy.

Setting off that morning, I reached the facility and inquired about her residency, only to find that she was no longer there, and no forwarding information was available. I thought that quite odd and frustrating. After that, I set out to the Hall of Records in San Diego, thinking the worst—that maybe my mom had possibly passed. I wasn't in touch with any of my family members anymore and did not know how to contact them for information.

Inquiring there at the Hall of Records, I came up empty-handed again. I was becoming frustrated and didn't know where to turn. I know there's many times that I acted as if I was very intelligent, but I really understand my own inadequacies at times. Then the realization came to me that my mother had been on SSI, so off I went to the Social Security office in downtown San Diego on C Street.

Walking into the office it was almost 4:00. The room was packed and lines were long, but to my amazement the line that I was in moved somewhat fast, and within a half an hour I was sitting before the man behind the glass.

As I sat down he asked how he could help me. I asked him to bear with me as I gave him the 5-minute version of what had transpired between my mother and I, and the experience that I had in prison, and how I was set out on a mission to reconcile with my mom. To my amazement the man did not even flinch as I told him the story. He did not throw me out of the office or act as if I was some kind of crackpot. He calmly listened and then began asking me questions as he got on the computer.

I remember him asking me for a place of birth. He asked me for Social Security number, even for her date of birth—none of which I had answers for. I only knew her full name. I felt like such an idiot not even knowing my own mother's birthday, and I remember him asking me, "You don't even know your own mother's birthday?"

I said, "No, I don't. My mother and I were never really that close."

As the clock ticked and it became closer to 5:00, the man sat there with me patiently. He even went as far as redirecting his line to another caseworker to help these people before closing time. There, he and I sat alone as he continued to ask me questions about her marriage with Mel and his whereabouts—unfortunately coming up with no information.

Sincerely thanking the man for taking the time that he did. There was that sinking feeling in my heart as I got up to walk away, but he assured me that he would continue working on this, and contact me, if there were any changes .

Walking out of that office, looking at all the cracks in the sidewalk, scraping my feet as I went down to the trolley, I boarded the train. Suddenly my phone rang. It was the man from the office. Asking if I was close by, I told him yes, I was just down at the trolley station. He said, "Come back. I think I found her."

Actually having to force the door open, I jumped off the train in excitement and scurried up to the office.

Entering the room, there he was all by himself with his face in the screen of the computer, while other lines remained. At this time it was almost 5:00. He waved me over, questioning me again and punching the keys on his computer.

He finally said, with the sigh of relief and excitement in his actions, "Yes, I found her. She's here in the San Diego area and alive. Unfortunately, I cannot give you any of that information, but I will forward your information to the facility where she's staying and they will contact you."

"That's great, that's awesome. I can't thank you enough for your time. I really appreciate everything that you've done, sir."

With a smile, he assured me what a pleasure it was to have helped me. I walked out of that room floating on clouds. I figured it would be a couple of days before I heard anything, but it didn't make any difference—I finally found her.

On the way home, I imagined the things that I would say to my mom. I imagined the situation in my mind and wondered how she was. I could see her face in my mind: black hair and black frame glasses, wearing those pastel muumuus that she always wore, with the horrible color patterns.

Walking into the house, the phone rang—and I mean right as I walked in the house. I was surprised. It was Mark Steingart, the coordinator from Sharp Coronado Hospital, informing me that my mother was there in the acute ward.

Explaining to me my mother had a stroke years ago. She was bedridden and had been there for four years on a feeding tube and tracheotomy, but that I was welcome to come see her.

All of that information was frivolous in my mind. I just wanted to know where she was located and if I could come see her now. Visiting hours were until 9:00 p.m.. I knew I could make it over there in time. It being 6:00 now, I told him I would see him shortly.

Turning right around, I walked back outside, caught the bus going back down to downtown, then transferring over Coronado Island.

Getting off the bus, it was just a short walk from the main highway over to Sharp Coronado Hospital. I remember looking at the quaint little houses there and thinking what a beautiful neighborhood it was. Anticipation began to rise in my senses, and I thought about all the time that had passed—all the hurtful words I had exchanged with my mom at times.

I recalled a particular time when I had been drunk and my mom was trying to keep me from getting in the truck to drive. As I ran away from her, she grabbed my collar, and I jerked away from her, sending her crashing to the ground—a moment in time that I'm not particularly proud of. It was all about defusing the situation and getting my way.

Entering the lobby, the hospital décor was retro—'60s and '70s laminated walnut, orange vinyl cushions, and fabric wallpaper. There were also the fake rustic brass fixtures in there, taking me back to a sense of my childhood growing up in the early seventies, but it had a good feel.

I was greeted by Mark Steingart and one of the nurses who had been caring for my mother. He explained the gravity of her situation, that she was heavily sedated because of her bedridden state. He warned me to brace myself, but I was fully prepared to see my mom.

Remembering the last time that I saw her—we were on the beach together with my wife and children. The horn frame glasses, the muumuus and her jet-black curly hair.

As I walked into the door of her room, I was taken back. She looked just like Grandma Celia—the one that she had told me we would see in heaven again. She didn't have any glasses on anymore, and the muumuu was replaced with a bed gown. Her hair was long and gray.

As I approached her bed, she was sound asleep. The scent of baby lotion emitted from her body, indicating to me that she was clean and well cared for. I touched her face. Her skin was soft, and her hair also. There was no response to the touch—just silence as she inhaled and exhaled.

I began to call to her softly, saying, "Mom... Mom..." but there was no response. I gently grabbed her hand and began to rub it and pat the back of her hand. There wasn't even a flinch. She was in a very deep sleep. I even went as far as shaking her shoulders every once in a while and calling her name, "Sammie."

Trying for about a half hour, I finally thought to myself that I would come back another day and just let her rest. Totally satisfied in the fact that I had found my mom finally, and that I knew reconciliation was just right there. Speaking out loud, I said, "I guess I'll just have to come back tomorrow," and headed toward the door.

Just as I was about to step out the door, something inside me said, Stop. Look back. And so I did.

As I looked at my mom I noticed tied to her bed were all of these helium balloons, and above the bed there was a banner that said, "Happy Birthday, Sammie Ellis, April 5th."

I couldn't believe it. The whole time that I had been standing there, fixated on her face, I never even noticed those balloons or that banner. I pulled out my phone, looking at the date—it was April 5th.

I literally looked up at the ceiling as if looking into heaven and said, " okay God, I get it."

Immediately, I turned around and went to my mother's bedside and began shaking her—not so gently, you might say. Somewhat violently. There was no way in the world that I could let this moment in time pass. Coincidence? I think not.

As I took her by the shoulders and yelled her name even louder and louder—"Mom! Mom!"—her eyes began to flutter. I continued to shake her and yell her name. As she began to open her eyes and squint, I said, "Mom, it's your son."

The look of confusion over her face—you could tell she still wasn't quite awake. It hadn't set in. Then I said, "Mom, it's your son, Raymond."

Immediately that look of confusion burst into the state of perception. Her eyes got wide, and her face just radiated with joy. Though she could not speak, the words that she spoke—or tried to speak—were very clear: "I love you."

Then she puckered her lips for me to give her a kiss, which I definitely reciprocated. The tears began to roll from her eyes and mine also. Just being in this memory right now, my eyes are welling up with emotion as if it were yesterday.

I told her how sorry I was and how wrong I was for being mad at her, and asked her to forgive me. I indicated to her that it made no difference who my father was or what the story was—that I wanted to leave all that behind us. It was very difficult to communicate with her, but that moment was priceless.

There were so many things that I wanted to say and so many questions that I wanted to ask, so I had to take control of the conversation and word it in such a way that she could either nod yes or no. I realized that she too must have had resentments or anger towards me. Frustrations. Pain. As a mother watching her son go down the wrong path.

I led her through many of these questions and thoughts, her indicating either yes or no, but she did indicate to me that she had resentments towards me for taking the path of a drug addict, how I had treated her and Grandma and Granddad throughout the years. Once again, tears welling up in her eyes as she wiped them away.

Sometimes frustration grew, because she was trying to communicate certain things to me, but it was almost impossible to get clarity on what she was saying. She was unable to write because she was unable to see with accuracy, but I'm not even sure that she would have been able to hold a pen at the time.

On a future visit, I thought about a man that had a tracheotomy and used one of those vibrating tools that you would hold against your throat to speak. I asked the staff there and inquired if it would be possible to get one of those so I could communicate with my mother. I remember them saying that all they had to do was deflate the cuff in her throat in order for air to pass through the larynx.

Somewhat animated, I said, well, why don't we do that? But the reality was that possibly her breathing could not be supported on her own, but they were willing to give it a try for my sake. They said that they had to run it by the director, which they did, and he agreed.

We set up a time for me to come in so that there would be a staff there, just in case something went wrong. Was great anticipation, that day came. Standing there, as they deflated the cuff in her throat, they asked her to speak, and for the first time in four years my mom was able to talk.

She coughed a lot because of the irritation in her throat, which was their great concern. If it persisted, they would have to inflate the cuff, but they would give us some time to try and talk things out. I called my Aunt Donna, and when she picked up the phone, I said somebody here wants to talk to you, and handed the phone to my mom.

As she whispered I love you, Donna just burst into tears. She said I love you too, Sammie. My Aunt Donna had guardianship over my mother while I was out of her life, but being the closest of kinship I was able to make some of these choices.

Donna was so excited to hear her voice. Somewhat let down, never realizing this option could be done over the many times she had come to visit my mom. As frustrating as it was, she was truly happy that I reunited.

The shameful part, looking back through all of these miracles, through all of these circumstances, and one of the greatest moments of forgiveness in my life, in making amends, I'm ashamed to say that I was still in my addictions.

I wish I could say that everything was perfect in my life from that moment on. That my mom and I spent every weekend together, but the fact is, I only visited my mom a few times more after that. I was still trying to maintain some kind of sobriety, dodging the parole board, and trying to get my life together.

I decided on the geographical cure one more time, leaving San Diego to go to Utah, taking a job in order to try and resolve this madness, this revolving door of addiction that I've been in. Finding temporal relief from my addiction, but my alcoholism ran rapid.

As painful as it was, I remember telling my mother. "I wish I could tell you, Mom, that I could take you away from here and take you from all this, and that you could live with me, but there's no possible way that I could ever give you the amount of care that has been given to you here, and my life is still incomplete."

I was very forward with her about my true state of being. I told her that once again I would be searching for serenity in my life, and that I had to live my life and find it. Although I knew it broke her heart, she understood, and with tears in her eyes, I said goodbye to her. I told her that I would come see her when I could.

I did take a paid vacation from Chapman Construction there in Utah, going to see my kids in Southern California and then dropping down into San Diego to see my mom one more time. After getting laid off in Utah because of recession in the oil fields, I then moved to Lake Tahoe, never to see my mother again.

Receiving the call about her passing one evening, I sat in deep reflection and guilt over never making time to go back down to see her. I projected her thoughts. Thoughts of the years she had laid in bed. How miserable it must have been, to be there imprisoned in your own mind, unable to care for yourself or even get up and walk away.

Relating the hours spent in regret over your life. Wishing what your life could have been, a pain that I can only somewhat imagine because of the imprisonment I have had in my own mind through my addictions. Thinking and dreaming of things I was going to do and never accomplishing because I could never be that far away from the bar, from the liquor store, or the connection.

Today I still talk to my mother, to her spirit, because I know that she still watches over me. I believe that our ancestors, our loved ones, are on the other side watching over us, waiting, caring, as I described in "The Promise."

I believe that we are cognitive on the other side. Mom, this is my amends to you. My acknowledgment of your Love in my selfishness. My release to you to live in peace on the other side. Knowing and acknowledging today. You gave me the best you knew how. I love you!

Chapter 6: The Bird

I remember the tremendous withdrawals I went through and not being able to stay awake. I slept for nearly a week only getting up to go to the bathroom and eat peanut butter and jelly sandwiches. Eight or nine every time I woke up and a gallon of milk. It seemed to be the only thing that would set well with my stomach. Everything else taste like sawdust. When I was able to finally stay awake, telling my grandmother I needed help, I found myself in the Care unit in San Bernardino California my first introduction to sobriety since the age of 10.

Unfortunately, I really did not understand the program, and the actual work that it took to achieve sobriety. I remember smoking a bowl of weed the very first day after getting out of treatment and the guilt and shame that proceeded. It wasn't long before I was drinking, smoking, and shooting cocaine and meth everyday.

Trying to find acceptance still, I got the bright idea that I would start dealing drugs. Everyone seemed to be my friend and I was well accepted as long as I had a bag. So that's what I did. I always sought out to get the best stuff. If it broke down in a spoon it was good if it left grit in the spoon it was crap. I didn't dabble with crap or at least I tried my best not to. At the age of 21, I picked up my first felony and was sentenced one year in the county lockup. This event was actually a life preserver thrown to me, that saved my life at this point. I was in such a bad physical condition probably weighing a little over 135 lbs. at 5'8". I couldn't do three push-ups. I couldn't do one sit up. I was definitely rescued. Sleeping for the first 2 months of my sentence, only to get up and eat, use the restroom and shower.

Finally, when I couldn't sleep anymore I became restless. Sending in requests to be a trustee, I would send a request in every day until finally, there I was working as a trustee in Riverside county jail in the kitchen. My body was starving. What a great place that was for me. Unfortunately, I went from 135 to 210 lbs. in 7 months at which time I was granted county parole.

Vowing to myself as I was released, I was going to change my life and not go back to drugs. Within 48 hours, I had an ounce of the strongest meth on the street at that time and I was off and running again. Getting my old job back as a meat cutter, it wasn't long before probation caught up to me, and I gave a dirty test. Thinking that I was going back to the old county jail, I prepared for the worst but my probation officer, or rather should I say God, working through him, gave me an opportunity to change my life.

He placed me in a place called banning road camp. A Riverside county jail facility in the city of banning California. There, I was able to enter a program called The second Chance program. At this time, it seemed funny it was called The second Chance program, because this was my second attempt at getting sober. A time which had lasting effects, and sculpted my way of thinking with certainty.

During my time at the Second Chance Program, in our living quarters in the barracks, there were pictures on the wall—one in particular, was a picture of Jesus standing with his arms stretched out. With a smile on his face, all the birds of the air had landed on him. In the background, you could see different animals, the lion, the lamb. I believe this is a fairly famous sketch of Christ. I used to marvel at it. Wishing I could obtain that power—that the animals would not be afraid of me and would come to me. Somewhat of a Grizzly Adams. I don't know if it was grandiosity or just admiration, but I thought it would be awesome. To have the trust of animals like that. I went as far as praying each night like a young child, that animals would not be afraid of me. I prayed that prayer for at least 30 days, maybe longer.

Outside of our barracks, stood two huge palm trees in which the birds would all make their nests. Four sparrows had fallen out at different times that spring, and they were unable to get back to the nest or into safety. There were feral cats around, so I picked the birds up, making a little nest for them under a milk crate. The birds were weak, and their plumage was not fully developed, so they were easy to catch—but difficult to feed. Their eyes were open, and they seemed terrified of this huge thing holding them, but reluctantly they would take the food. Eventually, they were strong enough to fly away, and they did so.

One day, I was in the bathroom doing my workout routine and brushing my teeth when I heard a huge commotion going on in the barracks. People were calling my name. I came out, curious what was going on, seeing a circle of guys gathered looking at the carpet. Everyone was yelling my name, telling me to hurry. They were laughing and saying, "Hey Fred! The word's out—free room and board at Barracks 11. Just go see Fred!" Inquiring what they were talking about, I approached the group. I looked down and saw this little bird. It looked like a miniature Thanksgiving turkey. It had three little feathers coming out of its tail, mulberries all over its beak and rear end, a wiggly neck, and closed eyes. The moment you touched it, it instinctively opened its mouth waiting for food.

Having pity on the little thing, I picked it up. It opened its mouth and chirping insistently, waiting. I made a little nest to keep it warm because it was absolutely featherless except for those three little tail feathers. I got some noodles and bread together and stuffed its crop full, since it was already evening. Once full, it went to sleep and stopped squawking. I put it outside the barracks because of facility rules, and placed a crate over it like a cage to keep the feral cats from getting to it. Covering it with a towel to keep it warm, I hoped I would find the little thing alive in the morning.

Early the next morning, The bird was still alive. Continuing to feed and care for it, days later, when it opened its eyes, that was it—I was mom, dad, whatever. I was everything to it. The bird and I were inseparable. As its plumage came in, my time was spent bouncing it on my hands to strengthen its wings. I'd walk barefoot in the yard, and the bird would follow me like a baby chick, pecking at my toes in a sewing machine fashion—it seemed like loving endearment.

Eventually, it was strong enough to fly and would perch in the trees outside the barracks. Sometimes it concerned me, wondering if it would come back. But all it took was a little chirp or whistle I'd developed, and it would respond. Sometimes the bird flew far—up to 300 yards—but I could always tell where it was by its trill, even when I couldn't see it. One call, and it would come swooping back toward the 14-foot razor wire fence, diving through it and landing on my shoulder or pecking my toes. In my mind, I can still see its little face, as it flew through the air towards me.

On my release day—July 9, 1993—the bird and I went to the dress-out area in receiving and release. The bird, tagging along; flying around the room and landing on the watch commander's logbook. Frustrated, the sergeant shouted, "You with the bird, you're first!" Jumping up, I thanked the bird, said "No problem," changed into my street clothes, and out the door we went.

My aunt greeted me outside with a little cage. I had been keeping them up to date over the phone, about the progress of my little bird, and being a bird lover herself, she was already equipped for the task. We drove to Calimesa, about 20 miles from the Banning road camp. After settling in and showing my grandmother the bird, I walked barefoot through the grass like I used to. The bird pecked at my toes again, chasing me through the yard.

Up until now I had been hand feeding my little friend, so I understood, teaching it to eat on its own was vital for its preservation. I kicked over a brick that had bugs and worms underneath, but the bird paid no attention. I then picked an apricot off a tree, and smashed it between my toes. Curiously looking at what was there between my toes, the bird approached, pecked, then eagerly ate the squished fruit. Understanding what I was trying to teach, it began pecking at the worms too. I knew then the bird would survive in the wild.

That afternoon I let it roam free in the trees. It chirped and sang with the neighborhood birds. I called it, and it would fly down and land on me, then fly back into the trees. That night, I caged it inside. The next morning, I let it out again, periodically checking on her, but that night I intentionally left her out.

But the next day, I called, but no response. I tried again over several days. Nothing. My bird was gone. I only hoped it was still alive.

Six months later, I saw an episode of America's Funniest Home Videos. One of the finalists was an elderly couple. In the clips, they were waving their arms yelling "Shoo! Shoo!" and a bird kept flying down to land on them. In the final scene, the old man held a female starling on his finger and said, "I've never seen anything like it." That was my bird. I knew it.

I always wanted to write the show and find out where the video was taken. I figue it was filmed in Banning, California. The bird must have flown back and found a sanctuary in one of those old retirees' yards. Without a doubt—it was my bird.

I think it was God's way of telling me the bird was okay. Instinct had taken over. It had gone home.

I don't know when I finally remembered the prayer I had made—the one where I asked God to make animals unafraid of me, like in the picture of Jesus with birds and lions and lambs gathered around. But when I did remember, I realized God had answered that prayer—just not right away. Looking back, I know God was always trying to tell me: "I hear you. I'm listening."

Today, I try to stay aware of how my prayers are answered—sometimes the same day, sometimes the next. But they are answered. I have no doubt. I challenge anyone reading this to put God to the test. I don't mean to ask for something outlandish, but even a little prayer—like mine for a bird—might reveal His power. He's waiting to show you. Just ask.

Chapter 7: The Portal in Time

In 2004, once again riddled with alcoholism and addiction—the reigning ruler of my life—I found myself seeking help through Set Free Christian Fellowship. I had been at the Cabazon Ranch for about six months and had served as the head overseer for approximately four of those. Despite being there for my own recovery, I was raised up to oversee the houses, guide the men, and be an example.

That always puzzled me. How could I lead while still so broken myself? But evidently, the pastor and others saw something in me that I couldn't yet see in myself.

I did my best to emulate the love of Christ and reflect what I was learning. I truly had a heart for ministry. I began to dream of evangelical missions and ministries—of living a life of purpose. But even in the midst of those dreams, my heart still ached for my family. This was just before I returned to Yucca Valley to try once more to reconcile with my wife—just before she married Patrick.

After my time at the ranch, I was sent to San Bernardino, where I was placed in a kind of spiritual holding pattern. For 30 days, I held no title, no responsibility—just time to reflect, to pray, and to let God work with me. Every day I sat on my bed, weary and uncertain, asking God the same prayer over and over:

"Is this what You want for me, God? Do You want me here? Should I leave? Am I in the right place?"

The same questions, day after day. Scripture says—paraphrasing—if you bug someone enough, they'll eventually give you an answer. I laugh now, but that's what it felt like: me pestering God.

Then one day, as I sat there on my bed praying that same prayer, with my eyes wide open, I saw it.

A portal began to open in the center of the room. It started as a small circle and widened until it was the size of a vanity mirror. I was looking through it—and what I saw was the same room I was in... but it was a different point in time.

I knew without a doubt that what I was seeing was real. There was no sound. No flash of light. Nothing to draw attention to it. But I saw it—clearly. And just as quickly as it had opened, the portal closed again.

I hadn't been drinking. I wasn't on drugs. I had been clean for eight months.

This wasn't a hallucination.

This was a vision—a message from God.

And the message was clear: I was exactly where I was supposed to be.

Be that as it may, I still got the thought in my head that I needed to be close to my family to reconcile with them—completely disregarding that vision and the letter my wife had written me, stating that she had moved on.

I still remember Pastor Ray urging me not to make that move—that God was perfectly capable and strong enough to reconcile that relationship right where I was, if He wanted it to be so. I ignored his warnings and had it determined in my heart that I was going to make it happen. But as you can see through the stories in this book, the timing was wrong. Things were off. God had not prepared the way, and thus things ended up the way they are.

I can only imagine the frustration that Pastor Ray must have felt. I know he indicated to me in our conversation that many others had gone out and done the same thing—made the same mistake—stepped outside of what God was trying to build into our lives. How frustrating it must be to see that happen time and time again.

Today, I stand outside the box. I can look into that portal in time, and I can see exactly what Pastor Ray was talking about. It wasn't until I surrendered again that things started to move in my life. God was allowed to manipulate the situations around me to bring the good gifts that He's always wanted for me. I had to put down self-will.

Maybe, just at this very moment in writing these words, I've been enlightened as to how self-will and God's will cannot coexist. It is only when our will aligns with His that peace and serenity become part of our fiber.

I recently saw a sermon that Pastor Ray gave on YouTube. I saw and heard a broken man. Obviously, he was experiencing the frustrations and disappointments that he saw in the people he taught and had the best intentions for. It broke my heart, and I burst into tears thinking about the man I looked at as a mentor—someone I still hold dear in my heart to this day.

I know the love he has for Jesus, for ministry, and for the saving of lives—trying to point people to Christ, not to anything he has, but to what Jesus has.

I hope that one day this book will land in his hands. Maybe it can rekindle a fire in his heart for the ministry. I remember him stating in that sermon that he didn't see that brokenness in the crowd anymore—the people who were truly touched by the Gospel of Jesus Christ.

I don't know what was going on—if it was some kind of challenge he was in, or if the people simply weren't receptive. Maybe there was no confirmation coming to him at the time—no indication that people were truly listening. I am so sorry to say that it has been 20 years since I stepped out of that ministry program, only to fall on my face because of my own ego. I thought I was going to go out there and do it on my own, but I ended up on a desert island in the middle of the sea, so to speak.

I was alone in the desert with no form of spiritual accountability. What a terrible place to be. But I do remember those words always resonating in my head: "God is able to restore right here where you are today, Fred."

And that's why I choose to stay exactly where I am today.

I thought about moving out and getting my own apartment—once again moving way too fast in early recovery. But I was finally able to have a moment of clarity and even bounce it off of my sponsor. He said to me, "Fred, you're in a good spot. God has directed you exactly where you are right now. Just stay there. Just continue to do the right thing, and God will open up the doors of opportunity for you at the right time."

He is the shadow—or the alignment—of Pastor Ray. Someone who is, and will always be, dear to my heart.

Thanks, Pastor Ray. A.K.A. Weebles.

Chapter 8: The Provision for My Children

In 1998, my wife and I separated.

Actually—if I'm being honest—I left. I was angry at the world. I took the kids' piggy bank, loaded my belongings into the truck, and walked out on my wife and three children—one of whom was my stepdaughter, whom I had loved and raised as my own since she was an infant.

I was furious at everyone and everything. I truly believed my family would be better off without me. But the image that's stayed with me—the one that still haunts me to this day—is the memory of those three little faces pressed up against the living room window, waving and smiling as I drove away. They thought I was heading off to work, that I'd be back later that night. They had no idea I wouldn't return. I still can't sit with that image for too long—it's a crippling kind of pain.

Seventeen hours later, I arrived at my cousin's house in Colorado Springs. I was welcomed with open arms, but the morning after I got there, I knew I had made the worst mistake of my life. I called my wife and told her that—told her I was wrong, that I shouldn't have left. She didn't hesitate.

"I told you," she said. "If you leave—don't come back."

And she meant it. She never changed her mind.

Still, I worked hard while I was in Colorado. I made good money and continued to provide for her and the kids even though I wasn't there. I bought her a van, helped with the bills, and supported her as she went to school to earn the credentials she needed to care for the family. I did it without hesitation. She was a good mother, and I loved my children. I wanted them to have what they needed.

Eventually, I moved back to California and tried—many times—to get back into my wife's good graces. I enrolled myself in anger management and sought therapy in Colorado before coming back, because I truly wanted to change. I was still carrying a lot of unresolved pain, particularly resentment toward my own mother, but I was trying.

Throughout those years, I prayed the same prayer over and over again: "God, please care for my children. Please provide for them in my absence." I must have prayed it hundreds of times.

I held onto hope that one day I'd be reunited with them.

One night, after I had returned to the area, in Yucca Valley, my wife and I went out to Sizzler. We had dinner, and I remember her sitting across the table from me, speaking with that old spark in her eyes. She talked about the kids and her life, and for a moment, something in me stirred. But in that very moment—looking across the table—I knew deep in my heart: I could never be the man she truly needed. Not then. Not for her, not for our kids.

I wanted to be there so badly, but I knew our being together again would be poison for all of us. And while I admitted that truth to myself, it didn't make it easier when she told me Patrick had proposed to her—and she had accepted.

I was crushed. And yes, I was furious.

I didn't know Patrick personally, but I remembered his kids. I'd even taught them in Sunday School. He had four children of his own and was raising them alone. She had three. Together, it wasn't quite The Brady Bunch, but close. Four and three. Still, I was bitter.

About a year and a half later, I was still praying that same prayer—still asking God to care for my kids. And one night, I had a sudden realization: God had answered my prayer a long time ago.

He had put Patrick in their lives. He had provided. He had cared for my children even when I couldn't. It was a hard truth—but a beautiful one.

That night, I called my wife. I told her I was happy for her. I told her God had answered my prayer—and I hadn't even realized it. The answer had been there the whole time, right in front of me. I was just too blind, too broken, to see it.

I wasn't able to be the father they needed... the husband she deserved... the friend she once had. But Patrick stepped into all those roles. And she was there for him, too. His kids needed a mother, and her kids needed stability. In my eyes—and in my heart—I believe it was all orchestrated by God.

Years later, when my daughter turned 18, I received an invitation to her wedding. She was getting married right out of high school. At first, I didn't think much about the ceremony or what it would entail. But that night, alone with my thoughts, it hit me—how could I possibly give her away? I hadn't been consistently present in her life. I had been in and out, just as my own mother had been in mine.

Patrick had been the rock in her life.

In my heart, I knew it was only right for him to walk her down the aisle. Ironically, a few days later, my daughter called me and said, "Dad, there's something I want to talk to you about."

"Sure, sweetheart," I said. "What is it?"

She was quiet, hesitant. Then she asked, "Would you mind if Patrick walked me down the aisle and gave me away?"

I told her immediately, "I think it would be an insult if he didn't."

She sighed in relief. "Thank you for understanding, Dad... I thought you would be upset, but you get the first dance."

I was elated. That moment meant the world to me. My deepest gratitude goes out to Patrick—for being that man. I hold him in the highest regard.

Thank you, God, for answering my prayer.

Chapter 9: My Heart Attack: Be Careful What You Pray For

I remember around Thanksgiving of 2023, I was sitting out in the desert in Nevada in my RV all by myself. I was looking around the RV and thinking to myself, "What a mess." Everything I start, I don't finish. I started this project—didn't finish it. Looked over at another—started another project—never finished it. I had just become a damn tweaker.

I was sitting there smoking and drinking and shooting dope, thinking about what a mess my life had become. And in my moment of brokenness, I sat down with the pipe in hand and started praying to God—and being specific. I said, "God, without sending me to prison, could you please intervene in my life and do something that would help me to change my life?" And I left it at that.

About 10 minutes later, I started having this pain in the middle of my back. I thought maybe it was a pulled muscle, because I've had that happen before. But as I sat there and started to stretch and move around, even massaging my back on the corner of the wall, it did not go away. In fact, the pain began to start in the middle of my chest. It felt like Hulk Hogan was squeezing me—front to back.

I remember saying, "No, no, no. This isn't what I meant!"—thinking about how I was trying to be specific in the prayer. Because if you're not specific with your prayers, usually God could use just about anything anyway—or any method—to change your life.

I was supposed to be back in Lake Tahoe that evening anyway to go to work, so immediately I knew I was in trouble. I had no phone reception out where I was, and the nearest hospital was well over an hour and a half away. I remember grabbing my bag and throwing it into my car, getting in, and heading toward Lake Tahoe. I passed my cousin's house and didn't use the phone there—even though they have reception because of Starlink—because I knew the ambulance would take forever to get there anyway.

So I headed toward Interstate 80. By the time I got to Rye Patch, I pulled over at the gas station and tried to lay down in the back of my car for a little bit, hoping that maybe the pain would subside. But by this time, the pain had increased and was in both arms.

I got into the driver's seat again and proceeded toward Lovelock. By the time I was 10 miles out of Lovelock, the road was very clear, and I was speeding down the freeway trying to get into town so I could go to the hospital.

Arriving at the hospital, I walked into the emergency room. It was very quiet—a ghost town. Nobody in there. Not even a receptionist or a nurse. I rang the bell and yelled, "Hello!" and it was several minutes before somebody finally came into the emergency room—a young nurse, 23 years old. I told her I thought I was having a heart attack, and she went into action. Got me into a room and started administering the medicines I needed for the pain and for the reduction in my blood pressure.

Within an hour, I was being flown to Reno, to Renown Hospital, where I stayed and was treated for three days. I was honest with them about my addiction and that I had sworn to change my life and to get help.

On my release, the first thing I could think about was getting a beer, though. I only managed to stay clean off of drugs for 30 days before returning to my addiction. But it definitely did change my mindset. And every time that I picked up from then on, guilt riddled me about using—knowing that my days were numbered if I continued.

During the 30 days, though, I was able to go to Southern California with a friend of mine on a trip in which I was able to meet up with my daughter for the first time since I saw her at her wedding. She had since been divorced but was going to be remarried again. I got the pleasure of meeting her new fiancé, Hunter, who seemed like a fine gentleman—a stable man whom my granddaughter loved. My granddaughter that I got to meet for the first time.

It was great to see them. My daughter had since become a registered nurse and was working in Palm Springs. I'm very proud of her. She's a lovely woman—inside and out—and a very caring woman.

Once again, making the empty promises. They weren't empty at the time that I made them, but they became that way as I returned to my addictions. I also vowed that I would stay in contact—also becoming an empty promise. I think I only talked to her a few times up until the final straw of my addiction in March of 2025.

Today, I try to contact her at least once a week—if not twice. Sometimes it's just a text message, just telling her that I love her and that I'm thinking about her. I think that I have talked to Rebecca more in the past three months than I have in the past fifteen years.

I was surprised to see a text message from her on Father's Day this year, wishing me a happy Father's Day before I even woke up. It made me feel good inside because that hasn't happened for many years—and rightly so, because I just haven't been there at all for her either.

My son still does not talk to me at this time, which does bother me—but I am not mad at him. It's much the same, I think, between him and I as it was between my mother and I. I was always in and out of his life until the time came when he finally just said, "I've had enough"—just as it was with my mom.

I do not hold any anger toward him because I know that God will one day reconcile our relationship, just as He did between my mom and I.

Chapter 10: The Final Straw

It is now February of 2025. One more birthday down. I'm now 55, still looking around the same beat-up RV—sometimes clean, sometimes a complete wreck. I was finally able to gather up over 30 days of clean time off drugs, but I was still drinking myself to death.

In the year since my heart attack, I was still strung out. I had managed to gain another high-paying job, destroy it, then picked up another and destroyed that too. Then, staying out in the desert, I picked up a low-paying janitorial job—but it was a job, and it brought camaraderie with other people, something I needed because I was going insane from loneliness in my addictions. I couldn't stand to be with myself. My head continually ticked and raked over what I'd become. I had no mirrors in my place because I couldn't stand to see who I was hanging out with.

I reflect back on a skit from Saturday Night Live where they announced Sony had come out with a human-like robot that exhibited the characteristics of a human so well that it even recognized its own image in the mirror. Then in the skit, David Spade emphasized: experts say though it recognizes its own image, it will not truly be human-like until it learns to hate the image it sees. As comical and cynical as that sounds, that's exactly the truth. My own image disgusted me.

I was constantly doing things trying to find peace and serenity. I ended up leaving the job in the desert and came back to the Sierra Nevada mountains, helping a friend open a bar and hotel in Sierra City, California. I was supposed to be helping him, but I think maybe I was more hindering him. He was an alcoholic himself and our friendship had become toxic. I was no team player—I was a wreck, pulling down a handle night after night, a thirty-pack a day, however much alcohol I could get into myself.

I came to the realization that I couldn't continue living like this one more second. I had to find a way out. I really felt terrible. I did have some chest pain, but I knew I wasn't having a heart attack—yet I played that up just to have a scapegoat, a way to get out without having to face the fact that I was a complete alcoholic and on a sinking ship.

I told my friend I thought I was having a heart attack and needed to go to the clinic in Downieville.

On the way down, I was screaming to God—not in anger, but pleading for Him to save me, to take my will and my life and steer the car, keep the wheel out of my hands, because I was going to wreck it. I was going to destroy my life if I had control one more time. I pleaded with him to either take my life, or take my life and change it.

I remember how David prayed in the Psalms and asked God to take his enemies out from before him and make his path straight and clear. That's exactly what I prayed that day. I said, "God, please put the people in my life to help me so that you can change my life, because I don't know what's good for me. I've proven that time after time. And I promise you I'll stay out of the way for what you want."

At the Downieville clinic, they put me in an ambulance and took me to Grass Valley. They ran tests and found I was hemorrhaging internally from all the alcohol. But for the first time in a long time, I felt safe. I was suffering from delusions—maybe some of them not—but I was paranoid and fearful, thinking people were out to get me. I never really understood how powerful alcohol can be during detox.

I knew I couldn't go back. I told them I didn't have a safe place and needed help. After overnight care, they arranged a ride for me to a place called Lotus 24/7 in Roseville, Placer County. I had never been to Roseville, but I didn't care—if I didn't know where I was, nobody else did either. I was dead set on changing my life.

Lotus was a 24-hour facility, just to get you off the street for a day. You were given the opportunity to wash up and do laundry. They had sandwiches, TV dinners, and a bed. The next morning, I got up and started making phone calls. To my amazement, Placer County had all kinds of programs. I just had to call 211, and the help started coming out of the woodwork.

Placer County provided a wonderful caseworker—her name I cannot disclose, but she knows who she is, and God knows who she is. I thank her all the time for her help and respect. She's been an instrumental part of my recovery.

I was granted one more night at Lotus and transferred to the Harbor House on Douglas and Sunrise. The old hotel was clean, welcoming, and stocked with food. Once again, God had provided. I couldn't imagine trying to recover while worrying about rent, food, hygiene, and community.

Not everyone took advantage of the program—but I had the advantage: the desire to excel. Within five days, one of the residents OD'd on fentanyl. Another resident and I gave CPR and Narcan and brought him back. His lips and face were purple—he was gone. But he came back.

Later, the man—Brett—told me the next person who revived him, he'd swing on them. How stupid is that? I was dumbfounded. But I still checked in with him from time to time. He's not a bad guy—just trapped in addiction. I only pray that one day Brett will open his eyes and see what God is trying to do in his life before it's too late.

One morning, while I was in the shower, I was washing my hair and saying a prayer. I asked God, "Please put the people in my path that You want me to meet."

A couple hours later, one of the caseworkers offered to take me to Walmart to do a little shopping. She said she only had limited time, so we had to make it fast. I agreed, and we went up to the Walmart off of Lead Hill in Roseville.

I hurried through the store and got my groceries. Upon reaching the checkout, I started putting them up onto the counter. The lady and I started going back and forth with conversation. As I reached to get the last bit of groceries out of my cart, I turned and looked up—and there stood a man.

I say this what they laugh, but the first thing I noticed, he had nice hair and was clean-shaven. He had a bright, inviting look on his face. I felt as if I'd known him before. I stuck my hand out and introduced myself. He looked at me puzzled, stuck his hand out, and said, "Hi, I'm Terry."

Quickly turning away from the man, I went to the counter and started to pay for my groceries. I could hear the curiosity in his voice as he stood behind me. He said, "So Fred, what are you doing today?"

I said, "I don't know. I'm on a new adventure."

Once again, curiosity in his voice: "What kind of adventure is that?"

I said, "I'm not really sure yet. I'm eight days sober today, and I'm waiting for God to reveal the rest of that to me."

Terry walked up very close to me and whispered, "Twenty-eight years sober in the fellowship of Alcoholics Anonymous."

At that moment, I knew he was God-sent. I had only been to one meeting in the Roseville area and hadn't seen anybody or been clear-headed enough to choose a sponsor. I knew that time would come—that I'd need a sponsor to work the steps and relieve myself of the turmoil I lived in my head.

I turned and looked at him and asked if I could get his number. He agreed. As I turned to the ladies behind the checkout stand, they were already running out the tape and handing me a pen—before I could even ask for one. I laughed, noticing they already understood what was going on in the exchange.

I got Terry's number and spoke to him just after checkout. He indicated to me that if I wanted to talk program, to give him a call. I agreed. I then introduced Terry to my caseworker, then we went on our way.

As we went out to the car, I couldn't help but laugh and look at my caseworker. I said, "This trip had nothing to do with grocery shopping."

With a big smile on her face, she laughed and said, "I know—you're right."

We knew it was something much greater than just grocery shopping. It was to feed the body, yes—but it was for that divine appointment to feed my spirit. And it was just that.

Chapter 11: The Here and Now

One day my sponsor directed me to the Big Book of Alcoholics Anonymous and he showed me this passage and wanted me to read this passage on pages 558 and 559 of the Big Book. But the one that stuck out to me the most was the very last paragraph, and it states:

"Above all, we reject fantasizing and accept reality. The more I drank, the more I fantasized. Everything I imagined—getting even for hurts and rejections—in my mind's eye I played and replayed scenes in which I was plucked magically from the bar where I stood nursing a drink and was instantly exalted to some position of power and prestige. I lived in a dream world. AA led me gently from this fantasizing to embrace reality with open arms, and I found it beautiful. For at last I was at peace with myself and with others and with God."

It was absolutely amazing because that's what I'd been praying for so long. You know, there's another scripture that says that when a man is at peace with God, even his enemies are at rest with him. And this is something that just ate at my soul all the time, because I just wanted to be at peace—with my enemies, with myself, and with God.

And that's where I am today. I don't know if my enemies are at peace with me or not, but I don't even worry about those things, because God is able to handle those things. Today, I don't have to worry about my past and the things that I've done. I accept those things that I've done. I was messed up. I was on drugs, I was on alcohol, I was not thinking right, I did not act right.

Sure, some of those things have deeply scarred me, but as I work the steps of Alcoholics Anonymous, I was able to let go of those character defects. I know what's right and what's wrong, and today, that's what I live. I've let go of the old man that I was, and I grasp onto a new morality, a new way of life, a new way of thinking.

I have new friends, and I don't wish any ill will on any of my old friends or enemies. I pray for those that have harmed me. I pray for those that I harmed. I pray for joy and blessings on people that I've despised—people that I've had resentment against. I want good things for their lives, just as I want for my own.

Truly, I can see how the teachings of Jesus are the makeup of this program. Jesus said, "Love the Lord your God with all your might and with all your strength," and to "love thy neighbor as thyself," and all the rest of the commandments hinge upon these two things. And how true is that? If you love God, and you love your neighbor as yourself, you don't want to cause harm to people. You don't want to steal. Those are my heart's desires today.

The Big Book tells us to not regret the past or shut the door on it. Today we can use those things that used to be our liabilities, and we can use those as assets to help other people—reaching out into the darkness and pulling people back into the light.

Sure, I wish that I'd made better choices when I was younger or in my life altogether, but that is not reality. The reality is I made poor choices. Today, I don't. I choose to do the right thing. I choose to make the next choice the right thing.

I do not fantasize about how my life could have been if I had made better choices. My life is the way it is because of the choices I've made. But the thing is, my life is beautiful because of the choices that I make today.

I don't look too far into the future, because future-tripping takes me out of the peace that I have in my heart today. I know that God is guiding and directing me in every step of my life. I give the credit to Him. These are not the things that I do—I just get to walk through it. It is a blessing and a peace that I've never understood before, and I know that it is there for every person for the taking.

People may think I'm a fanatic or I'm crazy for saying that, but it's true. And I see countless lives that are changed, that experience the same thing that I do—maybe some not all the time—but that's what I look for every day: just staying out of God's way and that peace that He brings to me, and knowing that He has my back.

I have food, shelter, clothing, and friends. All the rest of that is gravy. My basic needs are always met, I have a wealth of friends that are sober, that are good people striving to be better. I have a good job today. I have a car. I am independent, self-sufficient—and all because of God's blessings.

For a small season in my life, I've been under the umbrella of the funding of the State of California and Placer County. I'm truly grateful for their support—all the way from the housing programs where they have funded me to be in sober living environments into transitional living: California CalFresh, Medi-Cal, Placer County Action Team—all wonderful programs that have been designed to help people get back on their feet.

Something that I've used to change my life. I can only imagine what it would have been like to try and get sober if I had not had these programs—the pressure that I would have felt, having to provide for myself and make those bills.

Today, I get to let go of those programs and let somebody else have the opportunity to benefit from them. If you are struggling, reach out. 211 in the Sacramento area will put you in touch with people that can help change your life. All you have to do is just walk through it. There are people there that really care about your success. Don't think twice about it.

Next week, I get to start a lifelong dream—and I'm starting paragliding school. I'm excited, and I can't believe that I'm actually getting to do this—something that I would have just been a dream if I hadn't been sober. Today I set goals, and I get to accomplish them one by one.

When a bill comes in, I don't cuss and carry on about it. It is just one of those things in life—and I pay it. If you're reading this and it all just sounds overwhelming, don't look too far into the future. Just take the first step. And the first step is admitting powerlessness.

Reach out to God. He's listening. He's waiting for you to speak to Him. And sometimes it's just, "God, I don't know what to do with my life. You know what's better for me than I do. Help me. Put the people in my path to change my life." That's what I prayed, and that's how my life is. He does—He puts people in my path each and every day. Divine appointments.

My life is a living testimony of God's miracles. I hope and I pray that you get to experience the same.

Chapter 12: The Refiner's Fire (Epilogue)

In retrospect of my life, God has always been trying to remind me to be the best person that I can be. I know my grandfather was always trying to get me to be the best person that I could be. He put me in the boys' home out in Texas because I was throwing my life away. I thought the man was trying to punish me, but he was trying to save me from myself.

I remember the time that he came out to visit me after dropping me at that boys' home. He looked at all my awards on the shelves in my room, then turned with a face full of tears, gave me a hug, and said, "I knew you had it in you, son." It was only one of two times that I ever saw the man cry in my entire life with him—one of which was when his father died.

My granddad, on his deathbed, spoke a blessing and a curse over me. He said to me, "Son, you love good things. You love nice things in life. Either you're going to work hard and be straight and have nice things—or you're going to continue with the drugs and be a complete bum." And what a truth that was.

In Job 23:10, the scripture says:

"But he knows the way that I take; when he has tested me, I will come forth as gold." — Job 23:10 (NIV)

Job speaks about being refined—about coming forth as gold. When a person refines gold, he continually heats it, pulling the dross off the top—the impurities. And the moment the gold is completely pure, he knows it's ready because He can see His own image in it.

That's what God has been trying to do with me.

By no means have I led a life like Job or had the integrity that he had. But that, to me, is what God has been trying to do in my life: building that integrity—that purity.

As you go through various trials, don't grumble in anger. Maybe step back and look. See what God is trying to say to you. Maybe He's trying to let you know that He loves you. That He's trying to refine you—to be the very best person you can be.

Step back. See the miracles. Smell the roses. Take the time to stand in the Spirit—and come forth as pure gold.

About the Author

After years of suffering from addiction, through the grace of God and the program of alcoholics anonymous my life has completely changed from Total chaos to one of serenity and peace. Looking back at my life I can see how God has always shown himself to me and I want to share that hope for others to experience their own transformation

Read more at prayerworkspublishing.com.

www.ingramcontent.com/pod-product-compliance
Lightning Source LLC
Chambersburg PA
CBHW060425090426
42734CB00011B/2456